TRUMPET

Hymns FOR THE Master

15 FAVORITE HYMNS FOR SOLO PERFORMANCE

PLAYBACK+
Speed • Pitch • Balance • Loop

To access audio, visit:
www.halleonard.com/mylibrary

3705-2122-2055-2714

ISBN 978-0-7935-7189-5

HAL•LEONARD®

Visit Hal Leonard Online at
www.halleonard.com

World headquarters, contact:
Hal Leonard
7777 West Bluemound Road
Milwaukee, WI 53213
Email: info@halleonard.com

In Europe, contact:
Hal Leonard Europe Limited
42 Wigmore Street
Marylebone, London, W1U 2RN
Email: info@halleonardeurope.com

In Australia, contact:
Hal Leonard Australia Pty. Ltd.
4 Lentara Court
Cheltenham, Victoria, 3192 Australia
Email: info@halleonard.com.au

ALL HAIL THE POWER OF JESUS' NAME

Trumpet

Traditional

JOYFUL, JOYFUL WE ADORE THEE

Trumpet

Traditional

TAKE MY LIFE AND LET IT BE

Trumpet

Traditional

GOD OF GRACE AND GOD OF GLORY

Text by HARRY EMERSON FOSDICK
Music by JOHN HUGHES

Trumpet

BE THOU MY VISION

Trumpet

Traditional Irish

CROWN HIM WITH MANY CROWNS

Trumpet

Traditional

I LOVE THEE

Trumpet

Traditional

ALL CREATURES OF OUR GOD AND KING

Trumpet

Traditional

SAVIOR LIKE A SHEPHERD LEAD US

Traditional

Trumpet

Moderately

MY FAITH LOOKS UP TO THEE

Trumpet

Traditional

JESUS SHALL REIGN WHERE'ER THE SUN

Words by ISAAC WATTS
Music by JOHN HATTON

Trumpet

THIS IS MY FATHER'S WORLD

Trumpet

Words by MALTBIE BABCOCK
Traditional Music

slightly slower

rit.

FOR THE BEAUTY OF THE EARTH

Text by FOLLIOT S. PIERPOINT
Music by CONRAD KOCHER

Trumpet

WHEN I SURVEY THE WONDROUS CROSS

Trumpet

Words by LOWELL MASON
Music by ISAAC WATTS

AMAZING GRACE

Words by JOHN NEWTON
Traditional American Melody

Trumpet